Preventing Divorce

Greg and Candy McPherson

Bobb and Cheryl Biehl

MULTNOMAH

PORTLAND, OREGON 97266

Cover design by Bruce DeRoos

PREVENTING DIVORCE
© 1989 by Multnomah Press
Portland, Oregon 97266

Multnomah Press is a ministry of Multnomah School of the Bible,
8435 N.E. Glisan Street, Portland, Oregon 97220

Printed in the United States of America

Library of Congress Cataloging-in-Publication Data

Preventing divorce/Greg and Candy McPherson ... [et al.].
   p. cm.
  ISBN 0-88070-268-0
  1. Marriage—Miscellanea.   2. Mate selection—Miscellanea.
3. Communication in marriage—Miscellanea. I. McPherson, Greg.
  HQ734.P87   1989
  646.7'7—dc19   88-38559
                                    CIP

89 90 91 92 93 94 95 96 — 8 7 6 5 4 3 2 1

Preventing Divorce

*"Can two walk together,
unless they are agreed?"
(Amos 3:3).*

CONTENTS

INTRODUCTION

What are life's three most critical decisions?

The single most important decision any man or woman ever makes is the decision which will determine his or her ETERNAL DESTINY. How will I prepare for eternity? Will I choose to accept Jesus Christ as Lord and Savior, or turn in some other direction?

The second most critical decision a person makes in an entire lifetime is the choice of a LIFE PARTNER.

Many lives are lived in happiness—or misery—based on this single decision. The lives of our children and grandchildren, and ultimately how we feel about ourselves is determined in large part by this solitary choice. Choosing a marriage partner is the second most critical decision we are ever asked to make in life.

The third most critical decision we face in life is our career, WHAT WE WILL DO in light of the eternity ahead of us and the life partner beside us.

In one sense, all the rest of life's decisions can be seen as reflections of these three critical turning points.

The book you hold in your hands focuses on that critical second priority: a fulfilling marriage that will last a lifetime. Preventing divorce is what this book is all about.

We have a deep personal conviction that the agonizing, heart-wrenching process called divorce *can* be prevented.

We believe there are millions of couples worldwide, like ·us, who are sincerely interested in assuring that *their* marriage does not become just one more divorce statistic.

We also believe that couples want their marriages to go beyond just "staying together till the kids leave home." They want marriage to provide a rich intimacy not possible in any other relationship.

With this in mind, we have created basic questions designed to help couples share their thoughts, convictions, and preferences with each other. These questions cover 95 percent of the potential problems you may face as a couple. We have also included thirty-four questions specifically fashioned for engaged couples, and thirty more for the extremely "rocky" marriage.

The more you understand how your spouse (or fiance) thinks and feels about these issues, the more discussions you have, the more chance there is of your marriage lasting a lifetime.

If this book can give you new perspective on even a few areas in your relationship and help prevent the devastating effects of divorce on your life—one, five, ten, twenty years in the future—we will feel every hour we have invested was worth a thousand times the effort.

May God give you wisdom, patience, and understanding as you work your way through these relationship-building questions. Enjoy each other!

Greg & Candy McPherson
Bobb & Cheryl Biehl

HOW TO USE
THIS BOOK

The Red-Yellow-Green Concept

This is a practical tool designed to help you see where you are in the process of understanding each other. After you have thoroughly discussed a question, simply check the appropriate box in the margin: "R" (Red, for total disagreement); "Y" (Yellow, for different conclusions or for misunderstanding); or "G" (Green, for total agreement) . . . in pencil.

Your goal is to get to the point where you have many greens in each area of life, a sprinkling of yellows, and just a few reds. Once a question is "Green," you might even want to use a bright green marking pen or pencil to flag those questions—so you can see at a glance just how much you already agree on!

Some of the questions do not require that you agree; you're simply sharing personal experiences with each other. In that case, just mark it "Green" when you have finished your discussion.

Of the questions you mark "Red," there may be only two or three that could actually become marriage-threatening kinds of conflict. The chapter titled "How to Turn Red into Green" deals with that issue.

Talk It Out— Write It Out

One of the advantages of these questions is that you can simply talk them out. Depending on your personal preferences, you may even want to tape some of your answers to listen to yourselves in years to come. Think how your sons or daughters might value such an opportunity to hear your thoughts and feelings in twenty years!

If you are separated for periods of time because of career or school, you may want to write out your answers to pre-selected questions and send them to each other. In fact, this is a fun way to answer these questions even if you're *not* apart. Although it might sound like a lot of work at first, writing out your thoughts and feelings actually has many advantages. Writing gives you time to reflect on the question, to think about what you're going to say. You have a chance to give your answer in totality, without fear of interruption. Some people find it easier to *write* something very personal than to say it out loud.

How to Get Started

There are different ways you might approach these questions. Here are a few ideas:

1. Decide together on one of the seven areas that particularly interests you right now. Start with the first question, and work your way down, marking each Red, Yellow, or Green. As you answer the questions, make notes on your concluding thoughts in the book.

or . . .

2. Start with the first category (Financial) and proceed down the questions one by one, until you've answered them all. Then go to the next category (Marriage and Family) and do the same. Don't forget to mark each question Red, Yellow, or Green. Record your conclusions under each question.

or . . .

3. Answer three questions (or however many you decide) in one category. When those questions have been marked Red, Yellow, or Green, then go to the next area of life and do three questions from that category, and so on. Again, don't forget to record your concluding thoughts under each question.

However you do it, we strongly suggest that in each area of life you follow the questions *in order*. You will be surprised at the time you could waste trying to read ALL the questions every time you pick up the book! If you simply follow the questions in order, you will eliminate the hassle of trying to come up with the "perfect" question.

If you come to a question that doesn't seem to apply to your relationship, just skip it and move on. Or, if a question seems too sensitive to discuss at that moment, come back to it later.

As you answer each question you'll undoubtedly think of additional ones. Write them down before you forget them. (Someday you may publish your own book of questions!)

If you're not sure what the question means, just interpret it the way *you* want to.

Great Times and Places to Ask These Questions

- When you're taking a drive or caught in traffic.
- When you're home alone.
- At a pre-determined time each week (date-night, Saturday morning, Friday lunch, etc.).
- When you're having a romantic dinner.
- After a game of racquetball or tennis together.
- When you're taking a walk.
- When you're going on a picnic.
- When you're on a trip.

How to Get the Most Out Of Your Time Together

1. Receive each other's answers as you would a treasured gift.

Many of our parents stressed the importance of good manners on gift-giving occasions like Christmas and birthdays. They wanted us to learn how to express appreciation for the gifts that Grandma, Grandpa, and Aunt Hilda had purchased.

In the early years, the minimum requirement was a "thank you"—and maybe a hug or kiss. As you got older, you were probably told to look the gift-giver in the eye and put excitement in your voice, even if the gift wasn't exactly to your specifications.

Think how appalled your parents would have been if your response had been "Oh, no! This wasn't what I wanted!" or "Why did you get me this?" or "I already have one of these!"

What we need to understand is this: When the person you love agrees to go through these questions with you . . . when he or she is willing to share thoughts and inner feelings with you . . . *you are receiving a special gift*. A gift of time . . . a gift of vulnerability . . . a gift of love.

Obviously, then, the receiving of such a gift should eliminate comments like: "Why in the world would you think that?" or "Where did you ever come up with that idea?" or "That's the craziest thing I ever heard!" or "I don't agree with you at all. How can you possibly think that?"

If that's the way we respond, we're no different than the spoiled child at Christmas, displaying his disappointment verbally or by body language. We need to treat each other's thoughts, opinions, and feelings with a high degree of respect, taking care to respond with appreciation.

2. Keep the right attitude.

Remember . . . with attitudes, *you choose.*

There is a difference between "fair" and "intimate" relationships. In *fair relationships*, couples simply exist together, share minimal conversation, meet 50 percent of each other's needs, get along 50 percent of the time, and go the same direction as a team 50 percent of the time. In *intimate relationships* a man and woman really get to know each other. They learn how to identify and meet the majority (80 to 100 percent) of the spouse's needs, how to care and understand, how to deal with conflict, how to set goals together and work together 80 to 100 percent of the time.

> *PRINCIPLE: It takes 100 percent effort on each individual's part to work at building an intimate relationship.*
>
> *YOU CHOOSE . . . 100 percent effort, or less.*

Intimate relationships enjoy perpetual growth as they apply these primary attitudes. If these basic attitudes do not exist, you will probably struggle at building an intimate relationship. It will be like trying to drive a car with three wheels—at seventy-five miles per hour.

ATTITUDE #1—RESPECT

This is the opposite of being proud, arrogant, or know-it-all. It means being humble. Gentle. It means giving words and actions that demonstrate the value and worth you place on your spouse. It means causing your spouse to feel more important to you than other people or things.

> YOU CHOOSE . . . to show respect or disrespect.

ATTITUDE #2—TRUST

Honesty will cause your spouse to feel you are trustworthy. The way you treat your spouse in this area will demonstrate a sense of responsibility and care. An altitude of trust requires a willingness to be open to each other—not holding back your feelings just because you'd rather please the other.

> YOU CHOOSE . . . to be trustworthy or untrustworthy.

ATTITUDE #3—FORGIVENESS

An unforgiving spirit could put you in an emotional prison, causing you to become critical and negative. Unless you forgive, the hurt and the hate you might feel will never change. With forgiveness, healing can come—both to you and to the relationship.

YOU CHOOSE . . . to forgive or not to forgive.

Because your marriage relationship is separate and more significant than other relationships, the quality of these three attitudes in marriage should be greater than in any other relationship you have.

Some do's and don'ts for lifelong marriage communication skills.

DO:
- LISTEN—no interrupting.
- THINK BEFORE SPEAKING—don't rush words.
- SPEAK TRUTH—no exaggerating; be sensitive and loving.
- ADMIT FAULT—when you are wrong, seek forgiveness.
- RESPECT DIFFERENCES—your spouse has a right to a different opinion.

DON'T:
- QUARREL—if a disagreement becomes heated, back away until things cool off; then come back to talk.

- BE SILENT—open up, tempering your honesty with love and thoughtful wisdom.
- LET ANGER CONTROL YOU—when angry, state it, back away, come back gentle and thoughtful.
- CRITICIZE OR BLAME—choose instead to give support and encouragement.

A special note to married couples

You're going to enjoy going through these questions! It's never too late to sit down with your life partner and discuss these practical issues. Marking each question with a Red, Yellow, or Green light will let you see how many areas you agree on. It will also underline those areas which, under pressure, could be destructive to your marriage.

Your marriage is designed by God to last a lifetime. As you have probably discovered, a strong marriage rarely just "happens" on its own. On the contrary, it takes a lot of work, determination, willingness to learn and change, and a strong commitment by each partner.

If we could add one caution as you go through these questions, it would be this: *Don't make the mistake of assuming you know how your spouse will respond.* All of us are constantly changing. Each day, we become a slightly different person than we were yesterday. The change may be small—perhaps barely even perceptible. But it's there. You may *think* you know how your spouse feels about a question, but if it's been a while since you talked about it, that perspective may have changed!

That's why this book will be valuable to you for many years to come. As you keep notes in the book on your answers and conclusions, you may find it fun to go over the same question again in a couple of years to see if each of you still feels the same way about it.

Preventing Divorce will help you strengthen your marriage foundation. Plunge right in . . . and yes, you have permission to enjoy yourselves!

BASIC QUESTIONS FOR EVERY COUPLE

These questions are for everyone—those considering marriage for the first time and for couples already married.

SEVEN AREAS OF LIFE . . . NOT JUST ONE

One of the things you will quickly see in working through the questions is that they are broken up into the seven basic categories of life: Financial, Marriage & Family, Personal Growth, Physical, Professional, Social and Spiritual.

These seven categories have been listed alphabetically, but that doesn't imply that the first listed (financial) is more important, for example, than the last listed (spiritual). You really need a balanced discussion in *each* of the seven areas of life. Remember . . . record your conclusions

under each question and mark "Red," "Yellow," or "Green" in the margin.

A. FINANCIAL

One of the most frequent reasons given for divorce today is financial struggles and disagreements. To whatever degree a couple differs in their financial assumptions, it is highly likely they will experience a corresponding degree of strain in their marriage in this area. Simply discussing your financial assumptions will be extremely helpful in reducing the amount of tension.

1. How much income would you like to make this year? . . . in five years . . . ten years . . . twenty years?

☐ ☐ ☐

2. In today's economy, how expensive a house do you want to live in? . . . in five years . . . ten years . . . twenty years?

☐ ☐ ☐

3. What kind of car would you like to drive? . . . in five years . . . ten years . . . twenty years?

☐ ☐ ☐

4. How many dollars do we need to be spending on clothing a year? . . . in two years . . . five years . . . in ten years?

☐ ☐ ☐

5. How do you feel about what the children should inherit when we die?

☐ ☐ ☐

6. Do you feel children should be paid for jobs around the house? Why? How much?

☐ ☐ ☐

7. Do you feel our children should be given a car at age sixteen? Why or why not? If so, what kind of car . . . and for what reason?

☐ ☐ ☐

8. Do you feel children should be given an allowance? If so, how much at ages five, ten, fifteen, twenty-one? If not, why not?

☐ ☐ ☐

☐ ☐ ☐

9. How much money a year should we spend on luxury items such as jewelry, furs, athletic equipment, exotic leather goods, etc.?

☐ ☐ ☐

10. What percentage should we tip a waiter/waitress who has done an outstanding job? A poor job? A mediocre job? One who has been rude?

☐ ☐ ☐

11. How much should you have to pay to have your hair done? . . . cut? . . . permed? What percentage should we tip?

☐ ☐ ☐

12. If we inherited a million dollars . . . what would you want me to do?

☐ ☐ ☐

13. What is your personal philosophy about credit cards? Are you pleased or frustrated by my use of credit cards?

14.   What percent of our income should we give to the church? Why?

☐ ☐ ☐

15.   What percent of our income should we give to Christian organizations? . . . charitable organizations?

☐ ☐ ☐

16.   What percent of our income should we be saving?

☐ ☐ ☐

17.   How much life insurance should we have? . . . health insurance? What kind? What company?

☐ ☐ ☐

18.   Do you want to invest some of our money? How? When?

☐ ☐ ☐

19.   How do you feel about borrowing money from our parents or relatives?

☐ ☐ ☐

□ □ □   20. How do you feel about loaning money to our parents or relatives?

□ □ □   21. Imagine that a friend of ours borrows money from us and doesn't repay it. How would you feel? What would you want to do?

□ □ □   22. How much should we spend on a "get-away" weekend?

□ □ □   23. Do we need a second car? Do we need a different car? What kind? How much do you want to spend?

□ □ □   24. How would you have the maximum amount of fun if we only had two dollars to spend some evening?

25. How much should we spend on special occasions like:

Birthdays

_____ _____ each other's
_____ _____ parents
_____ _____ children
_____ _____ friends
_____ _____ others (you name)

Anniversaries

_____ _____ our own
_____ _____ parents
_____ _____ friends, relatives
_____ _____ others (you name)

Other Special Days

_____ _____ Mother's Day
_____ _____ Father's Day
_____ _____ Valentine's Day

Christmas

_____ _____ each other's gift
_____ _____ parents
_____ _____ children
_____ _____ brothers, sisters, nieces, nephews
_____ _____ co-workers
_____ _____ neighbors
_____ _____ clergyman
_____ _____ Christmas tree
_____ _____ decorations ☐ ☐ ☐

□ □ □ 26. Who should do the gift-buying for birthdays? . . . for anniversaries? . . . for Christmas? . . . other special days? (If it's usually the same person, how can the other one help?)

□ □ □ 27. How do you feel about declaring bankruptcy? Is it ever okay?

□ □ □ 28. What should our "dollar limit" be on purchases made without the other's knowledge? Why?

29. Prioritize the following household items as to their importance to you:

(#1 would be the first thing I'd buy; #2, the second, etc.)

_____ Dishwasher
_____ Compact disc player
_____ Washer/Dryer
_____ Color TV
_____ Microwave
_____ Food processor
_____ Food dehydrator
_____ Freezer
_____ Stereo system
_____ VCR
□ □ □ _____ Video camera

30. If you had the cash, which would you buy first, second, etc.?

_____ Dining room furniture
_____ Master bedroom furniture
_____ Living room furniture
_____ Expensive hobby items
_____ Piano
_____ Expensive athletic equipment
_____ Other   □ □ □

31. How much per month should I spend on clothing? How much per month should you spend on clothing? □ □ □

32. How much do you expect to pay for the following?

A. A pair of shoes
B. A shirt or blouse
C. Pants or slacks
D. Underwear, socks, or hose
E. A winter coat
F. A watch
G. Haircut
H. Medical check-up   □ □ □

33. What are your feelings about our (a) monthly budget plan? What changes could we make? What should stay the same? Are you pleased or frustrated by how we handle our money?

☐ ☐ ☐

34. What are your feelings about our "last will and testament"? What changes or additions need to be made?

☐ ☐ ☐

B. MARRIAGE AND FAMILY

You are not only marrying a single person of the opposite sex, you are marrying:

—your future mother-in-law

—your future father-in-law

—your children's other parent

—your future nieces and nephews . . . and all of the rest of your in-laws

—one of your grandchildren's other grandparents.

The success or failure of your marriage impacts a lot of people. Communicate honestly and clearly on these issues . . . there is a lot of family future resting on your discussions.

1. What does the phrase, "Till death do us part" actually mean to you?

2. Do you see divorce as an "option" for any circumstances?

If so, for what circumstances would you see it as an option?   ☐ ☐ ☐

3. What would you do if I became totally incapacitated and could never have sex or children?   ☐ ☐ ☐

4. What would be your response if I developed cancer or broke my back and was partially paralyzed?   ☐ ☐ ☐

5. What if our marriage doesn't turn out to be quite as fun as you expected it to be?   ☐ ☐ ☐

6. What if my job would require me to be away from home a week or two at a time? Do you feel you could handle being alone that much . . . without being tempted to "run around"? Do you feel I could handle being alone?   ☐ ☐ ☐

☐ ☐ ☐   7. How do you feel about me going "out with the boys or girls," (of the same sex)? How often?

☐ ☐ ☐   8. When we disagree with one another, how should we settle it?

☐ ☐ ☐   9. How did your mother view marriage?

☐ ☐ ☐   10. How did your father view marriage?

☐ ☐ ☐   11. What words would you use to describe your parents' marriage and relationship? Why? Your grandparents' marriage?

☐ ☐ ☐   12. If there has been divorce in your immediate family . . . what preventative steps can we take to avoid these similar patterns in our relationship?

Red Yellow Green

13. What are the three things you admire most about each of your parents as a marriage partner?

☐ ☐ ☐

14. What are the three things you admire most about your parents as people?

☐ ☐ ☐

15. What couple, that you know personally, has the most ideal marriage? Why do you think of it as so ideal?

☐ ☐ ☐

16. Ideally, how many children would you want to have? Do you have preferences about how many boys . . . how many girls?

☐ ☐ ☐

17. How do you think you would respond if we had a severely handicapped child?

☐ ☐ ☐

18. How would you respond if one of our children was severely injured and had to have months of therapy and extensive surgeries?

☐ ☐ ☐

Red Yellow Green

19. What should the five most strictly en-
forced rules of our house be in the area of
child discipline?

☐ ☐ ☐

20. What could I do to help you in the area
of parenting?

☐ ☐ ☐

21. What three things are (do you expect
to be) most rewarding about parenting?
. . . Most frustrating?

☐ ☐ ☐

22. How do you feel about spanking children? Under what conditions? How? With
what?

☐ ☐ ☐

23. What do you think about having our
elementary-aged children in Sunday
school or church? . . . junior high-aged?
. . . high school-aged?

☐ ☐ ☐

24. Do you feel elementary-aged children should be in a public or private school? What about home schooling?

     . . . junior high . . .

     . . . high school . . .

     . . . college . . .

Why?   ☐ ☐ ☐

25. What five to ten foundational scriptural truths do you feel should be stressed in the raising of children?   ☐ ☐ ☐

26. At what age should a son begin to date? When should a daughter begin to date? What would be your house rules for curfew?   ☐ ☐ ☐

27. What style of discipline would you use with a toddler? . . . elementary-aged child? . . . junior higher? . . . high schooler? . . . college-aged son or daughter?   ☐ ☐ ☐

28. How much of a child's college education should be paid by the parents? Under what conditions?

29. How much freedom/responsibility should children be given at age five? . . . age ten? . . . age fifteen?

30. What are the five things you definitely want me to do for and with our children?

31. What do you see as your role as a parent with our children? . . . My role?

32. How often should parents get away from babies in their first year, leaving them with baby-sitters, and getting away as a couple? . . . when the kids are older?

33. How do you feel about nursery schools? How do you feel about day-care centers? What are the advantages? Disadvantages?

☐ ☐ ☐

34. If it's Easter Sunday, and you want a new outfit, and the baby needs a new outfit, and you can only afford one . . . who would get the new outfit, and why?

☐ ☐ ☐

35. How much would you guess it costs to care for a baby per month in the first year? (You may want to double check with a couple who has a new baby, to see if your guesses are anywhere in the ball park).

☐ ☐ ☐

36. How do you feel about birth control, and what method do you see as being the ideal one for us?

☐ ☐ ☐

☐ ☐ ☐

37. How do you feel about male or female surgery to avoid having more children? At what number of children, or under what circumstances, would you consider it necessary to take precautions to not have any more children?

38. Who do you consider responsible to do the following work around the home:

A. Dishes _____
B. House cleaning _____
C. Picking up around the house _____
D. Yard work _____
E. Getting the cars fixed _____
F. Dealing with insurance _____
G. Getting the Christmas Tree _____
H. Fixing things around the house that go wrong _____
I. Making the bed _____
J. Washing clothes _____
K. Ironing clothes _____
L. Picking out what the kids will wear _____

☐ ☐ ☐
M. _____ _____
N. _____ _____

☐ ☐ ☐

39. How do you feel about an unmade bed in the middle of the day?

40. How often do you feel people should take showers? Brush teeth? Change the bathroom towels? Vacuum? Dust? Wash the tub out? ☐ ☐ ☐

41. How often do you feel it's important to go out for dinner, rather than cook at home? ☐ ☐ ☐

42. Who should do the cooking in our home? What kind of meals? Who should do the grocery shopping? ☐ ☐ ☐

43. Describe your ideal week of evenings. What would you do Monday night . . . Tuesday night . . . Wednesday night . . . etc.? ☐ ☐ ☐

44. How do you want to celebrate (in general) our wedding anniversary each year? ☐ ☐ ☐

☐ ☐ ☐ 45. Is there something fun or special you've always wanted us to do, but we haven't yet had the money or taken the time?

☐ ☐ ☐ 46. Would you classify me as a good listener to other people? To you?

☐ ☐ ☐ 47. What are three of your happiest memories of our life together so far? Why?

☐ ☐ ☐ 48. Are there areas in which we may be a bad example to our children?

☐ ☐ ☐ 49. Is it important to you that we go to "marriage seminars" or classes together? Why?

☐ ☐ ☐ 50. What are your feelings about abortion?

51. What has been our most fun vacation for you so far? Why? Do you prefer vacations spent visiting relatives, or vacations by ourselves? Why?

☐ ☐ ☐

52. What are your feelings about integration? What would you do if one of our children wanted to marry someone of another race?

☐ ☐ ☐

53. What changes would you want to make from your own childhood and teenage years in relation to raising our family?

☐ ☐ ☐

54. If one of your parents became widowed or sick, what would you feel our responsibility should be to him/her? If one of *my* parents became widowed or sick . . . ?

☐ ☐ ☐

55. What's involved in "romance" for you? (Be specific.) How important to you are those elements in our marriage?

☐ ☐ ☐

C. PERSONAL GROWTH

Remember back ten years . . . talk about what life was like for each of you a decade back. Ten years ago, could you possibly have imagined where you would be today?

If there is one thing you can bank on in life, it's the fact of change. Both of you may have the desire to grow rapidly over the next ten years . . . but *how* do each of you want to grow? In what areas? Where do each of you feel encouraged, frustrated, or held back?

1. A year from today, in what three to five areas would you most like to be stronger than you are now?

☐ ☐ ☐

2. In what area would you *most* like to grow (Spiritual, Physical, Personal Growth, Marriage & Family, Social, Professional, Financial) in the next ten years?

☐ ☐ ☐

3. In what three areas would you most like to see me grow in the next year? Why?

☐ ☐ ☐

4. What do you feel are the three key things keeping you from reaching your full potential as a person today?

☐ ☐ ☐

5. If you could become the "world expert" in any one area or subject . . . what would it be?

☐ ☐ ☐

6. In what area would you suggest I specialize and become an expert?

☐ ☐ ☐

7. What moral/social/political issues (i.e., abortion, war, rape, drugs, etc.) would you like to know more about? Why?

☐ ☐ ☐

8. What five books would you most like to read? Why?

☐ ☐ ☐

9. What seminar would you most like to attend? Why?

☐ ☐ ☐

10. If you could sit and chat with any person in the world . . . with whom would you talk? What three questions would you ask? Why?

☐ ☐ ☐

11. What do you consider your three greatest strengths to be maximized in the future? Your single greatest strength?

☐ ☐ ☐

12. If we could improve only one aspect of the way we relate to each other . . . what area would you want to work on? Why?

☐ ☐ ☐

13. What keeps you from getting excited about being promoted at work or taking on more responsibility?

☐ ☐ ☐

14. What negative comment did someone make about you several years ago, which is still holding back your confidence? How can I help you overcome that blockage in your life?

☐ ☐ ☐

15. In what three areas of your life do you feel you have grown most in the last three years?

☐ ☐ ☐

16. What three people have had the greatest impact on your life? Why?

☐ ☐ ☐

17. Name five of your all-time favorite books. What was it about each of these that you liked? Would you like me to read them?

☐ ☐ ☐

18. Who was your best friend in grade school? . . . junior high? . . . high school? . . . college? How did they contribute to your personal growth at that time of your life?

☐ ☐ ☐

19. If you had four hours in which you could do anything you wanted to do, what would you do? Why? If you had a weekend?

☐ ☐ ☐

☐ ☐ ☐

20. What single question do you keep asking yourself the most in the past few weeks?

D. PHYSICAL

One basic reality in life is that *we all change physically as we grow older.*

What are your thoughts about your own physical appearance and that of your life partner? How do you actually feel about your weight, your sex appeal, and your overall image?

☐ ☐ ☐

1. What three things do you find most attractive about my body?

☐ ☐ ☐

2. What are your taboos or things you do not want to do at all in lovemaking?

☐ ☐ ☐

3. Are you happy with our physical relationship? Why? What are your hopes for our lovemaking a year from now? . . . in five years? . . . in ten years?

4. From your perspective, what are the five most important things to be aware of when making love?

☐ ☐ ☐

5. What are the lessons you have learned (as much or as little as you know) from your parents' love life?

☐ ☐ ☐

6. How do you feel about an exercise program for you and me? What kind? How often?

☐ ☐ ☐

7. What events in your past do you think influenced your sexuality as you now experience it?

☐ ☐ ☐

8. How important to you are the following in lovemaking?

(1 - Crucial; 2 - Somewhat important; 3 - Not necessary for my enjoyment)

_____ A. Personal hygiene
_____ B. Foreplay
_____ C. The setting
_____ D. The amount of time available
_____ E. The limitation of distractions
_____ F. Creativity and positioning

_____ G. Perfumes, oils, candles, etc.
_____ H. Romantic conversation
_____ I. Garments
_____ J. Lack of tension
_____ K. Physical energy
☐ ☐ ☐ _____ L. No unresolved arguments

☐ ☐ ☐   9. What five things do you like best about my physical appearance, in general?

☐ ☐ ☐   10. What three suggestions would you like to make about how I can improve my physical appearance?

☐ ☐ ☐   11. In what areas would you like to improve your physical appearance?

☐ ☐ ☐   12. How do you feel about taking vitamins and nutritional supplements? How much per month should be spent on them?

13. Would you prefer to go to a medical doctor or a nutritionist?

☐ ☐ ☐

14. How do you feel about going to chiropractors?

☐ ☐ ☐

15. How do you feel about the food we eat? What changes would you make? Are you willing to help implement changes? (Shopping, cooking, studying, etc.)

☐ ☐ ☐

16. I have some anxiety about the following health problems in the future, based on my family medical history. (Specify.) How would you feel about me if I developed some of these?

☐ ☐ ☐

17. How do you feel about me being ten pounds overweight? . . . twenty pounds? . . . fifty pounds? How do you feel about you being ten pounds overweight? . . . twenty pounds? . . . fifty pounds?

☐ ☐ ☐

Red Yellow Green

☐ ☐ ☐

18. How do you feel about baldness? . . . wrinkles? . . . gray hair?

☐ ☐ ☐

19. How do you feel about image? Would you prefer (in public) I have a modest image? A sensual or provocative image?

☐ ☐ ☐

20. Is it a desire of yours to belong to a recreational club, such as the YMCA, or country club? Why?

☐ ☐ ☐

21. How do you feel about getting older? . . . 30? . . . 40? . . . 50? . . . 60? . . . 70?

☐ ☐ ☐

22. What do you plan to do specifically to avoid the potential of having an affair?

23. How do you prefer I would wear my hair? How do you feel about beards, mustaches, side burns? How many buttons should I leave open on a shirt or blouse? How do you feel about wearing bras?

☐ ☐ ☐

24. What is your favorite outfit/clothing, and why do you enjoy it?

☐ ☐ ☐

25. What kind of physical exercise would you most like to do together . . . and separately?

☐ ☐ ☐

26. What type of physical exercise would you most enjoy doing in summer? . . . in winter?

☐ ☐ ☐

27. What five nationally visible personalities do you most identify with personally . . . and would most like to be like?

☐ ☐ ☐

28. What five nationally visible personalities do you find most attractive to you personally, sexually . . . and what is it about them that you find attractive? How will you deal with the difference between what you find attractive in others of the opposite sex, and what I am not?

☐ ☐ ☐

29. What turns you off sexually? What turns you on sexually?

☐ ☐ ☐

30. How do you feel about alcoholic beverages? . . . smoking cigarettes? . . . mind-altering drugs?

☐ ☐ ☐

31. How honest are you about your sexual needs? Would you like to be more open? What can I do to help?

☐ ☐ ☐

32. What are your feelings about pornographic magazines, movies, etc? Explain.

E. PROFESSIONAL

As a person matures, he or she moves through phases like: "I got the job!" . . . "I think I'll choose this field as my profession" . . . "My career is progressing well . . . or, my career is in a slump" . . . "What will my life work be?"

As you each progress in age and professional experience, it is critical that both of you make the same assumptions concerning work.

1. How do you feel about my work? What do you like best about it? What about my work frustrates you? ☐ ☐ ☐

2. What do you think I would be very best at for a life work? ☐ ☐ ☐

3. What would you consider my top three alternative positions? Why do you feel these would be good things for me to pursue? ☐ ☐ ☐

4. To what association(s) should you, or I, or we belong? Why? ☐ ☐ ☐

☐ ☐ ☐ 5. How would you feel about my working with the _____ company?

☐ ☐ ☐ 6. What do you consider to be the five most important ingredients in bringing you happiness at work? How many of those ingredients are present in your position now?

☐ ☐ ☐ 7. What professional goals will you have to reach to feel successful in life?

☐ ☐ ☐ 8. What brings you the most *satisfaction* in your job/career? Job relationships?

☐ ☐ ☐ 9. What kind of work brings you personal fulfillment?

☐ ☐ ☐ 10. How important to you is the feeling that you are making a significant difference in your work?

11. How would you describe the difference between having a job, a profession, a career, a life work?

☐ ☐ ☐

12. How important to you is having fun on your job?

☐ ☐ ☐

13. How important to you is being a member of the team at work? How important is being accepted by that team?

☐ ☐ ☐

14. What will you have to learn, do, or become before you are ready for the next promotion at work?

☐ ☐ ☐

15. What role does *security* play in any career you would choose? Why?

☐ ☐ ☐

16. What would have to be a part of your profession/career for you to consider your job your life work?

☐ ☐ ☐

17. Which of the following would you like to do at work, if you had a choice:

A. Solve problems in totally original ways, but never have to do the practical work of carrying out your ideas . . . Why?

B. Have a combination of creating original ideas, but developing the first prototype . . . Why?

C. To be given a prototype or a model and have someone say, "Your challenge is to pioneer this idea in many new areas." Why?

D. To be given a work area where your area of responsibility needs a lot of debugging to refine it to the point where it's running smoothly . . . Why?

E. To be given responsibility in an area that is fairly smooth and running well when you take it over . . . and your role is to keep it running smoothly and possibly expand it . . . Why?

☐ ☐ ☐

18. If you were on a team and all the members of the team were approximately equal in ability and experience, and the pressure was on to make a directional decision on behalf of the team, would you—in your

heart of hearts—prefer to (1) be the captain of that team, or (2) a strong player on the team, giving input to the captain, but letting the captain take the final responsibility? Why?

☐ ☐ ☐

19. How do you feel about a career for me that would include travel? How much would be acceptable? How much would be unacceptable?

☐ ☐ ☐

20. How important to you is our parents' acceptance of what I do as a profession? . . . our children's acceptance?

☐ ☐ ☐

21. Would you rather work with your hands, your head, or your back?

☐ ☐ ☐

22. If you could have anyone's position in the world, whose position would you have, and why?

☐ ☐ ☐

□ □ □   23. What do you definitely and absolutely *not* want in your life work?

□ □ □   24. How would you feel about us working together as a two-person team at some point in the future? If you would feel good about that . . . what would you see us doing together?

□ □ □   25. In your heart of hearts . . . how do you honestly feel about a wife having a very separate career from her husband, where she may need as much support to keep going in her profession as the husband would in his?

□ □ □   26. How would you feel about me making more/less money than you . . . if that should happen?

□ □ □   27. What is it in a job, profession, or career that you would definitely *not* want me to be a part of in the future?

28. If I had all the time, energy, and money I needed and could have any position in the world . . . what position would you ideally like me to have? Why?

☐ ☐ ☐

29. If my work responsibilities required me to make a move, in what parts of the country/world would you feel comfortable living? In which parts of the country/world would you definitely *not* want to live?

☐ ☐ ☐

30. If my career required a move and yours did not . . . how would we decide what to do?

☐ ☐ ☐

31. If I, as the husband, made enough money so that you would not have to work outside the home, would you still want to work, and why?

☐ ☐ ☐

32. If you (the husband) were out of work . . . or did not make enough money for us to have the niceties we wanted as a couple . . . how would you feel about me, as your wife, working and supporting the family?

☐ ☐ ☐

☐ ☐ ☐ 33. How do you feel about the wife working outside the home when we have pre-school children at home? . . . elementary school children at home? . . . junior high children at home? . . . high school children at home? . . . college-age children at home? . . . when we are empty nesters?

☐ ☐ ☐ 34. How would you feel about me working swing shift? . . . graveyard shift?

☐ ☐ ☐ 35. How would you feel about me working two jobs?

☐ ☐ ☐ 36. How do you think your father feels (felt) about his work? How do you feel about his work?

☐ ☐ ☐ 37. While you were growing up, did your mother work outside the home? Either way . . . how did you feel about it? Why?

38. If you ever had a position in which you were very happy, but got fired . . . how would you want me to relate to you when you came home from work?

☐ ☐ ☐

39. What is the highest position you can imagine me holding at some point in the future?

☐ ☐ ☐

40. How would you feel about me if I became a:
. . . factory worker?
. . . doctor?
. . . lawyer?
. . . rock singer?
. . . movie star?
. . . farmer?
. . . truck driver?
    salesman?
. . . businessman?
. . . company owner?
. . . clergyman?
. . . missionary?
. . . psychologist?
. . . police officer?
. . . politician?

☐ ☐ ☐

41. What if the career I chose required me to do three to ten years of preparation before I could become successful. How would you feel about that long of a waiting period?

42. How would you feel about me, if after five years of working hard in some business enterprise or profession, I failed in that profession?

43. How would you feel about starting a company from scratch, where there was a major risk of the money we invested from our savings?

44. Would you prefer that I be on a lower fixed salary, or a higher potential commission, with no guaranteed income? Why?

45. If I decided to go back to school for continuing education, how would you feel about that decision? Why? What would be the advantages? Disadvantages?

46. What company, organization, or firm would you most like to work with if you had your ideal preference? Why?

☐ ☐ ☐

47. If you could start a company with anyone . . . what three people would you choose to be your partners? Why?

☐ ☐ ☐

48. If you were to start a company of any kind . . . what kind of company would you start? Why?

☐ ☐ ☐

49. Would you hesitate to start a company of our own? Why?

☐ ☐ ☐

50. How would you define the position that would absolutely maximize all of your greatest strengths, as clearly as you can see them today?

☐ ☐ ☐

F. SOCIAL

Friendships are invaluable!

Social times are priceless!

But, are both of you making the same assumptions about your social lives? Do you really enjoy the same people, going to the same parties, or entertaining in the same way?

□ □ □ 1. How do you really feel about parties? What kind of parties do you most enjoy? Least enjoy? Want to avoid at all costs?

□ □ □ 2. How confident do you really feel, socially, on a scale of one to ten, where "one" is insecure and "ten" is extremely confident?

□ □ □ 3. What is the best party you've ever attended, and why did you enjoy it?

4. Who are your five closest friends, and why do you enjoy them? Who are five casual acquaintances you'd like to have as close friends someday, and why? Who are five people you used to have as friends, but have drifted from? Why did those

friendships drift, and how does it make you feel when you reflect on them?

☐ ☐ .

5. When going out for a social evening, what do you enjoy doing most with another couple or small group of people?

☐ ☐ ☐

6. How do you feel about tent-type camping?

☐ ☐ ☐

7. How do you feel about having friends "pop in?" . . . your relatives? . . . my relatives?

☐ ☐ ☐

8. How do you feel about us "popping in" on friends? . . . your relatives? . . . my relatives?

☐ ☐ ☐

9. How do you feel about having out-of-town friends stay overnight with us? . . . out-of-town relatives?

☐ ☐ ☐

10. How do you feel about staying with friends when we travel?

11. If we were to take a trip with another couple, within five hundred miles of home . . . what would you want to do? How long would you want to stay? Where would you want to go? . . . With whom?

12. How many nights a month would you be open to guests staying in our home?

13. What qualities do your friends share in common? What do you look for in a friend?

14. What do you give to a friendship, or to a social relationship?

15. Where should we meet new friends? (Church, work, family, etc.)

16. What puts pressure on you socially? Why?

□ □ □

17. How do you feel about your parents' social life? How do you feel about my parents' social life?

□ □ □

18. How would you improve on either one of our social lives?

□ □ □

19. Who do you consider your top ten lifelong friends—friends you'd like to remain close to twenty, forty, fifty years from today . . . and why in each case? How do I feel about each of your close friends?

□ □ □

20. What are the social situations in which you feel least comfortable, and why?

□ □ □

21. What are the social situations in which you feel most confident, and why?

22. What do you most enjoy doing on an evening out? Why?

23. What are the elements of a social event that make you frustrated? . . . disappointed? . . . angry? . . . uncomfortable?

24. If you could go to any "high society" event in the world . . . what event would you most enjoy attending? Why?

25. If you could go back in history to any social event that has ever happened on the face of the earth . . . what social event would you most enjoy attending? Why?

26. If we were given two thousand dollars to go somewhere just for fun . . . where would you go? Why?

☐ ☐ ☐

27. If we had only twenty dollars to do something "wild and crazy" together socially . . . what would you do? Why?

☐ ☐ ☐

28. If we had two hundred dollars to spend socially . . . how would you want to spend it?

☐ ☐ ☐

29. What kind of parties do you most enjoy? (Theme parties, costume parties, Valentine parties, Christmas parties, New Year's parties, etc.) Why?

☐ ☐ ☐

30. If we were to go to dinner on five separate evenings, with five couples who are married . . . what five couples would you most enjoy going to dinner with? Why in each case?

☐ ☐ ☐

□ □ □ 31. If we were to go with one couple to some foreign country in the world . . . what foreign country would you want to visit? . . . with whom? Why?

□ □ □ 32. How many evenings a week or a month would you enjoy socializing with friends as a married couple? Why?

□ □ □ 33. What do you give to a friendship?

G. SPIRITUAL

The two areas which are American taboos of conversation are politics and religion. In marriage, however, these topics are "must discussions!" The Bible warns about being "unequally yoked" or being of different faiths. Take your time and discuss each of these questions as openly as possible. Ten years from now you will be extremely pleased you did!

□ □ □ 1. When you lean back in your chair and imagine heaven . . . what do you see?

2. How do you feel about church in general?

□ □ □

3. How often would you like to attend church?

□ □ □

4. Is our church meeting your spiritual needs? Why or why not?

□ □ □

5. What do you enjoy giving . . . doing . . . being involved in at church?

□ □ □

6. What does the Bible mean to you personally?

□ □ □

7. How often do you actually read the Bible? Why?

□ □ □

☐ ☐ ☐   8. What does prayer mean to you?

☐ ☐ ☐   9. How do you feel about our having devotions together? Why?

☐ ☐ ☐   10. How would you feel about my being a member of the clergy someday? Why?

☐ ☐ ☐   11. Discuss three highlights of your spiritual life?

☐ ☐ ☐   12. What was a low point of your spiritual life?

☐ ☐ ☐   13. To you, what are some important biblical issues, principles, or doctrines? Why?

14. If you could ask God any three questions . . . on any topic . . . what would you ask? Why?

☐ ☐ ☐

15. How do you see marriage and divorce from a biblical perspective?

☐ ☐ ☐

16. How do you feel about . . . think about . . . Jesus?

☐ ☐ ☐

17. In what area of your spiritual life do you feel the greatest need for personal growth?

☐ ☐ ☐

18. From your perspective, what are three keys to a strong spiritual life?

☐ ☐ ☐

19. If I felt "led of God" to move to Africa and work with tribesmen . . . what would be your reaction?

☐ ☐ ☐

☐ ☐ ☐   20. What is the single most meaningful part of your spiritual walk?

☐ ☐ ☐   21. Is there anything separating you from God?

☐ ☐ ☐   22. What do you believe about heaven and hell?

☐ ☐ ☐   23. What does a "commitment to God" mean to you?

☐ ☐ ☐   24. What do you believe is God's standard regarding sex within marriage, and sex outside of the marriage bond? Do you agree with it? Why?

☐ ☐ ☐   25. If I want to determine God's will when making a major decision, I usually follow this pattern . . .

26. From a biblical perspective, what do you see as the husband's responsibility to his wife? . . . to his children? . . . to the spiritual welfare of his wife and children? In each area, what are examples of practical ways you see this responsibility being carried out in our marriage?

☐ ☐ ☐

27. From a biblical perspective, what do you see as the wife's responsibility to her husband? . . . to her children? . . . to the spiritual welfare of her husband and children? In each area, what are examples of practical ways you see this responsibility being carried out in our marriage?

☐ ☐ ☐

QUESTIONS ESPECIALLY FOR ENGAGED COUPLES
(Or Those Considering Engagement)

The best time to decide whether you will live the rest of your life together is *before* you say "I do" . . . not after!

Today, couples considering marriage are more reflective, and in fact, more cautious about the marriage decision than couples fifteen to twenty years ago. That's good . . . particularly if a couple has the right tools and solid premarital counseling.

This book will be a significant tool for you to honestly evaluate your relationship. Any engagement which cannot stand the asking of these questions indicates a high likelihood the marriage could not stand the pressure of living in today's society.

It is *far* better to break an engagement (as hard and embarrassing as it would be at the time) if there are major unresolved differences than to go to the divorce court after the marriage vows have been spoken and the children have been conceived.

It is not the purpose of this book to break engagements. It is our desire to simply bring to light areas of existing agreement and disagreement, giving you time to fully explore your disagreements.

Of the numerous questions in the Basic Questions for Every Couple, and in the following questions for engaged couples, you may find only *two or three* questions that are potentially "engagement-breaking" disagreements. These you can then talk through prior to proceeding with the wedding.

But let's suppose you put off the critical discussions on these issues until *after* marriage . . . until *after* the children have arrived . . . until *after* major financial commitments. Then let's assume some major problem arises and one of these three areas of disagreement must be discussed under the pressure of financial deadlines, career choices, or sick children. These are the situations in which marriages come apart.

We want to help both of you find the partner you'll be happy with for the rest of your life. We also want to do everything we possibly can to help you prevent divorce. It is our hope that these questions will assist you to make a wise, clear-minded decision in choosing a life partner . . . till death do you part.

Remember . . . these questions are to be used in addition to the Basic Questions for Every Couple.

A. FINANCIAL

1. Do you see both of us working after marriage . . . and if so, for how long? ☐ ☐ ☐

2. What is your philosophy about credit cards? Do you abide by that philosophy? How many do you have now? What are the debts on each? Which cards should we have after marriage? ☐ ☐ ☐

3. Do you see yourself as a "saver" or a "spender"? Why? ☐ ☐ ☐

4. Will our income after marriage support the standard of living you've become accustomed to? If not, what adjustments are you willing to make? ☐ ☐ ☐

☐ ☐ ☐ 5. What are your financial obligations right now (other than credit cards)?

☐ ☐ ☐ 6. Who's going to write the checks for bills to be paid?

☐ ☐ ☐ 7. For the first year of our marriage, do you want to live in a house, apartment, mobile home, condominium, or tent? Why?

☐ ☐ ☐ 8. How much money should we spend on furniture the first year? Why? Cash or credit card? What are your feelings about buying used furniture?

☐ ☐ ☐ 9. What are your feelings about joint versus separate checking accounts?

10. How much money do you currently spend on clothing each month? $ _____   ☐ ☐ ☐

11. How much do the following cost you?
    pair of shoes _____
    shirt or blouse _____
    pants or slacks _____
    underwear, socks,
      or hosiery _____
    dress or suit _____
    winter coat _____
    cosmetics _____   ☐ ☐ ☐

12. What are your feelings about a "will"? When do you think we should have one made? Why?   ☐ ☐ ☐

B. MARRIAGE AND FAMILY

1. What do you feel my future relationship should be with friends of the opposite sex—friendships I had prior to marriage? (Name each one specifically—especially past romantic relationships—and discuss each of your assumptions about those relationships.)   ☐ ☐ ☐

□ □ □ 2. How do you feel about premarital counseling? Why? What are the advantages?

□ □ □ 3. What would be the advantages of waiting one more year to get married? What would be the disadvantages?

□ □ □ 4. How long do you feel we should be married (as an adjustment period to life together) before having children?

□ □ □ 5. Who should do the cooking in our home? What kind of meals? Who should do the grocery shopping?

□ □ □ 6. Are you a night person or a morning person? How would you account for any differences in those two conditions?

7. How should a couple spend a Saturday? How should they spend a Sunday?

☐ ☐ ☐

8. What are your five most positive expectations about our married life together?

☐ ☐ ☐

9. What are your five greatest concerns or lingering questions about our married life together? Who could we talk to that would help us understand and deal with our concerns prior to saying "I do"?

☐ ☐ ☐

10. Where are we going to be at Christmas? Thanksgiving? Mother's Day? Father's Day? My birthday? Your birthday?

☐ ☐ ☐

11. What if we were not able to have children?

☐ ☐ ☐

☐ ☐ ☐ 12. Do you foresee any of our relatives interfering in our marriage? Who? How?

☐ ☐ ☐ 13. How does your mother feel about our relationship? . . . your father? . . . your brothers and sisters?

☐ ☐ ☐ 14. What do you picture us doing on our first vacation?

☐ ☐ ☐ 15. Are there any skeletons of *any kind* in your past? (I want no surprises after saying "I do" . . . bankruptcy . . . homosexual activity . . . child abuse . . . prison time, etc. We should talk about these things before the final commitment—*not* on our honeymoon!)

C. PHYSICAL

☐ ☐ ☐ 1. What are your three favorite thoughts about making love after marriage?

2. What are your three greatest concerns about making love after marriage?

□ □ □

3. What are your standards for our physical expression before marriage? From what source do you get your standard?

□ □ □

4. What are five assumptions you have about how I will make love?

□ □ □

5. Do you have a favorite recreational activity? How often do you participate in it now? Does it require continual updating of equipment? How much do you spend in a year on that activity?

□ □ □

6. How much fresh air do you like when sleeping? When you use an electric blanket, do you set it closer to 1 or 10?

□ □ □

D. SOCIAL

☐ ☐ ☐ 1. How would you guess our social relation-ships (with each of our current friends) will change when we get married?

☐ ☐ ☐ 2. One year after we are married . . . what difference would you anticipate in our so-cial life? Five years after? Twenty years after?

E. SPIRITUAL

☐ ☐ ☐ 1. How strong are your parents' religious convictions?

☐ ☐ ☐ 2. Do you tithe (give 10 per cent of your income) regularly to your church? Do you plan to continue tithing after marriage? Do you think a tithe is based on net or gross income?

☐ ☐ ☐ 3. What denomination is important to you? Why? Is there a particular church or de-nomination you would *not* want to be in-volved with? Why?

QUESTIONS FOR COUPLES CONSIDERING REMARRIAGE

You may have already been through the agony of divorce. We have thought much about you as we have written this book. We have heard many stories in counseling sessions and know how desperately you want your next marriage to "make it."

You need to know that we do not agree with divorce. We do not believe divorce is the answer. But for those of you who find yourselves in this agonizing situation—even though you didn't choose it—we want to help you address some difficult but absolutely important issues and questions before you decide to remarry.

You may have lost your partner through death and are trying to survive the bouts of loneliness, the frustrations of handling things alone. Remarriage sounds so good at times but so scary at others.

Your experience tells you to proceed with caution. Don't be afraid to listen to that little voice. Don't ignore those yellow flags. Don't be pressured to move too fast. Take the necessary time to talk, observe, listen, and pray.

Maybe you should, maybe you should not remarry. It is our prayer that these extra questions will be key to helping you make the right decision. In addition to answering these questions, we recommend that you read Dr. Charles Swindoll's booklet *Divorce* (Multnomah Press, 1980) for sound biblical counsel on the subject.

A. FINANCIAL

☐ ☐ ☐ 1. What are your financial obligations relating to alimony and child support?

☐ ☐ ☐ 2. What kind of outstanding debts and other financial obligations do you have? What is the amount owed on each debt?

☐ ☐ ☐ 3. How would you feel about paying bills that my former spouse created, and I am now obligated to pay?

4. What was the financial settlement from your divorce? May I see your divorce papers?

☐ ☐ ☐

5. How would you feel about facing financial pressures that may develop in the future relating to my previous marriage? (i.e., How would you feel if we end up in court several more times, and it costs $5,000 each time?)

☐ ☐ ☐

6. What are your feelings about a prenuptial agreement? Do we need one to protect ourselves and our assets? (A prenuptial agreement is a written legal statement made *prior* to marriage stating your intentions regarding each of your assets, debts, etc.)

☐ ☐ ☐

IF THERE ARE CHILDREN INVOLVED:

7. How would you feel about paying child support for children who won't be living with us, and who may not even accept you?

☐ ☐ ☐

8. Where should the child support money go? (Into a general fund, a separate checking account specifically for the child, etc.?)

□ □ □

9. Do you think we need a prenuptial agreement to protect your children's inheritance? . . . my children's inheritance?

□ □ □

10. Are you willing to pay for counseling for my children? . . . your children? . . . children who don't live with us?

□ □ □

B. MARRIAGE AND FAMILY

1. What are five reasons, besides love, that you want to marry again?

□ □ □

2. What are your feelings about living in "his" or "her" house? Would a new "neutral" house be better for us and the children?

□ □ □

3. What are your parents' feelings and attitudes about your divorce? . . . About your former spouse?

☐ ☐ ☐

4. What are three causes of your marriage break-up?

☐ ☐ ☐

5. How are your parents responding to our relationship? Your friends?

☐ ☐ ☐

6. Would you want us to have children? Why? Are you physically able to have children?

☐ ☐ ☐

7. How has your philosophy or theology of marriage changed since your divorce?

☐ ☐ ☐

8. What are your top three fears about our relationship?

☐ ☐ ☐

☐ ☐ ☐   9. Are you willing to be accountable to a third person (clergyman, counselor, etc.) concerning our relationship?

☐ ☐ ☐   10. What are your feelings about seeing my "ex"? . . . About talking with him/her on the phone?

☐ ☐ ☐   11. What are your top three fears about remarriage?

☐ ☐ ☐   12. What three-to-five things did you do that may have contributed to the break-up of your marriage? What would you do differently now?

IF THERE ARE CHILDREN INVOLVED:

☐ ☐ ☐   13. Do you feel your children should be involved in your decision to marry? Why? How much?

14. What about child custody . . . is it final? What are the existing arrangements? What are your feelings about it?

□ □ □

15. Would you be willing to adopt my children if the opportunity arose? Why?

□ □ □

16. Assuming I have custody of my children, are you willing to love, raise, and financially support my children (your step-children) *alone* in the event I were to die? How does that make you feel?

□ □ □

17. If we were to get full legal custody of my children in the future, how does that make you feel? Why?

□ □ □

18. Are you willing to face any future problems that may arise, and the related stress (financial, emotional and physical) concerning visiting rights/custody of my children? Why? How would you deal with this?

□ □ □

☐ ☐ ☐ 19. What should our plan be when we see or sense the children trying to cause a conflict between us?

☐ ☐ ☐ 20. How can we keep from "playing favorites" with the children?

☐ ☐ ☐ 21. How would you maintain a "fairness and balance" concerning the discipline of the children? . . . concerning the amount of money spent on each?

☐ ☐ ☐ 22. Who should handle discipline of the children? What has been your style in the past? Spanking? Grounding? Privileges taken away? Nothing?

☐ ☐ ☐ 23. What might you do if your child doesn't want to obey me—and comes running to you?

24. How do you feel about those who are complete strangers to you (i.e., the children's "other" grandparents) having strong influence over our family's holiday and birthday schedules and plans? ☐ ☐ ☐

25. How much input or "say-so" do you allow your children in family decisions? ☐ ☐ ☐

26. How might you feel when my children talk about my former spouse? ☐ ☐ ☐

27. Are you willing to put me first, even before your children? Will you purposefully choose me, above all relationships, even at the expense of the relationship with your children? Why? ☐ ☐ ☐

28. How would you feel about my children being involved in the wedding ceremony? . . . your children? ☐ ☐ ☐

☐ ☐ ☐ 29. Are you willing to give up the "honeymoon" phase? In other words, do you understand that our break-in time to marriage will be very limited, because we have children? How does that make you feel?

☐ ☐ ☐ 30. What are your children's sleeping habits? Are they used to sleeping with you in the same room? . . . in the same bed?

☐ ☐ ☐ 31. What kinds of food and beverages are your kids used to eating? Junk food? Fruits and vegetables? Simple meals? Gourmet meals? What kinds of changes do you feel need to be made?

☐ ☐ ☐ 32. Are you prepared for the potential hostility of my children getting "bad press" about you from my former spouse's side of the family? How might you handle it?

☐ ☐ ☐ 33. What kinds of manners and attitudes would you expect from your (or my) children around the house? At mealtime?

34. How do you think your parents (or other family members) will react to unknown children now being a part of their family? How could we help them adjust? □ □ □

35. How do you feel about arguing in front of the children? Because of your past marriage, are there certain types of behavior that are frightening to your children? (Loud voices, swearing, ignoring each other, etc.?) □ □ □

36. What are your expectations when it comes to family vacations? Do you want children to go with us? What about children who don't live with us? If they come, who pays their way? □ □ □

37. What traditions are you or the children used to at Christmas? . . . birthdays? . . . Fourth of July? . . . other times? □ □ □

38. What traditions do you feel must be kept? What are new traditions we can start? □ □ □

39. What are your expectations regarding the way our children will treat each other? Are you hoping (expecting) that they will love one another as "blood" brothers and sisters? What is your plan to help them adjust?

☐ ☐ ☐

C. PHYSICAL

1. What methods of birth control are you willing to use in the future? Why?

☐ ☐ ☐

2. You most likely developed certain expectations and hopes regarding sexual relations in your past relationship. These same expectations are often carried over into the new relationship. What are your expectations and hopes regarding our sexual relationship? What do you feel is normal sexual behavior? How often are you expecting to have intercourse?

☐ ☐ ☐

3. Are you willing to have a physical exam and a blood test? An AIDS test? If not, why?

☐ ☐ ☐

4. If you have had a vasectomy, are you willing to consider a reversal? Why?

☐ ☐ ☐

5. Have you experienced any sexual difficulties in your past marriage relationship that could affect *our* sexual relationship? (Lack of desire, impotency, etc.?)

☐ ☐ ☐

6. How do you feel about communicating on sexual issues? Embarrassed? Awkward? Comfortable? Why?

☐ ☐ ☐

7. How demonstrative of our physical relationship do you think we should be in front of the children? (Holding hands, kissing, hugs, etc.)

☐ ☐ ☐

8. Was there infidelity in your past marriage?

☐ ☐ ☐

9. How could we help our children understand, accept, and control their potential sexual attraction to their stepsisters, stepbrothers and/or stepparent?

☐ ☐ ☐

D. SOCIAL

1. How would you handle being "scrutinized" and "evaluated" by my friends? . . . by my family?

☐ ☐ ☐

2. How might you handle potential resentment from my friends or relatives directed toward you over our relationship? How could I help?

☐ ☐ ☐

3. What are your feelings about us making new friends who aren't connected to our past marriage(s)?

☐ ☐ ☐

4. What are your feelings about attending social events that I also attended with my former spouse?

☐ ☐ ☐

5. Thinking back to couple friends from our previous marriages, which do we feel comfortable continuing to see? ☐ ☐ ☐

6. Are there any of our friends who would likely feel uncomfortable seeing us? ☐ ☐ ☐

E. PERSONAL GROWTH

1. In what areas do you feel potential frustration, anger, or bitterness: your financial settlement? . . . property settlement? . . . children? . . . reputation? . . . loss of family unit? . . . other? Why? What are you doing to resolve these feelings? ☐ ☐ ☐

2. What is there about your past lifestyle that you would not want to give up? ☐ ☐ ☐

3. How would you describe your self-esteem level right now? Low? Fair? Healthy and confident? Why? ☐ ☐ ☐

□ □ □ 4. What would help strengthen your self-esteem? (Self-esteem consists of your sense of *worth*, your sense of *belonging*, and your sense of *competence*.)

F. PROFESSIONAL

□ □ □ 1. How do you feel about me working with people who knew (know) my former spouse? How much pressure does it put on you? How can I help?

□ □ □ 2. Would you be willing to relocate or change jobs if necessary if I found it hard to adapt?

□ □ □ 3. Are there any "hard feelings" or resentment about your divorce among any of your co-workers? How do you handle it?

4. The following are seminars, meetings, etc. that I am required (or expected) to attend. Of those, these are the ones that my spouse is expected to attend with me. What are your feelings about that? ☐ ☐ ☐

G. SPIRITUAL

1. How do you think God views your divorce? ☐ ☐ ☐

2. Are you willing to have a clergyman evaluate our present relationship? . . . my previous relationship? ☐ ☐ ☐

3. How would you adapt to attending church where my former spouse attended? What are your feelings about finding a "neutral church? ☐ ☐ ☐

4. What are your feelings about us committing our marriage to God? What does that mean to you? ☐ ☐ ☐

☐ ☐ ☐   5. How have you reconciled your divorce situation with God? . . . with yourself?

☐ ☐ ☐   6. What are your expectations regarding family Bible reading and prayer?

☐ ☐ ☐   7. Remarriage is regarded by many Christians as adultery. How do you deal with that stigma?

HOW TO TURN A RED LIGHT TO GREEN

(What If We Don't Agree?)

The first thing to ask yourself is: "Is this an important issue to me? To us?" If your difference of opinion is on something *both* of you consider insignificant, then forget it! You don't need to read any further. Go back and enjoy answering some more questions and discovering more about each other.

However . . . if the red light is over an issue of significance to *either one* of you, consider:

A.   "There is more than one way to skin a cat." In other words, there is more than one conflict-resolution skill or approach available.

We will not list them all for you. Our objective is to give you a few ideas on how to approach the conflict. They may or may not work for every "yellow" or "red" issue you are dealing with; but hopefully you will be able to make headway toward a "green."

B.   If these ideas do not work, we suggest that together you seek a qualified pastor or counselor. Let your counselor see what you have discussed so far regarding the issue.

Unfortunately, many times either the man or woman won't even *consider* talking to a pastor or counselor . . . that is, until one or the other announces they're leaving the relationship. *Then* the reluctant one is willing to talk, but in many cases it's too little, too late.

It's a wise couple who is willing to put pride behind them, and seek the qualified help of a good counselor early on. Don't wait for the storms to come before you test the ability of your boat to float.

Ideas to consider

You cannot resolve a difference if one partner chooses to be passive and silent.

You cannot resolve a difference if one partner chooses to be less than 100 percent involved in making it work.

You can certainly live together without "red lights" resolved, but your relationship will be weakened . . . and possibly vulnerable to an affair or potential divorce.

Here are three CONFLICT-RESOLUTION approaches anyone can use. These should help you take significant steps to close the gap. In each of these approaches, skill in communication is extremely helpful.

1. BARGAINING—In this solution, each person looks for a meeting point some place between the two of them where both can agree. Each person must be willing to offer some sacrifice, but neither should do all the sacrificing.

If bargaining is used to manipulate, withhold, or punish the other partner, it wlll not work! It your relationship has not practiced or developed open, honest communication, the chances of "playing games" wlth this technique will be compounded.

Remember: Three attitudes must be cemented into your marriage foundation: *respect*, *trust*, and *forgiveness*. An agreement reached through fair bargaining should remain relatively solid through the passing of time. If re-bargaining is required, stay open to that possibility. In the meantime, do all within your power to nurture and support the agreement.

2. CARING CONCESSION—In this approach, one partner acknowledges the disagreement, yet chooses to go over to the other partner's side. The objective of the acquiescing partner is to close the distance between them, to bring harmony and one-mindedness back into the relationship.

If the motivation for this action is control, or the decision is made because of coercion, the agreement will probably not hold up.

The best motivation for one partner to totally surrender to the wishes of the other—without consideration of his or her own wishes—is love. Anything less than this will probably not be strong enough to sustain a solid relationship. Caring concession and love gifts are good reasons to acquiesce. But if one person *always* gives while the other generally takes, then this kind of agreement is not solid. There needs to be a just balance of give and take.

3. AGREE TO DISAGREE—There are some conflicts or disagreements that, for the present, seem to be irreconcilable. If this situation presents itself, you need a way to accept, at least for a time, the fact that the disagreement resists resolution. In order to maintain respect and trust between the two of you, agreeing to disagree is workable only as long as it is understood that the issue is put on the back burner *for now*. This is not intended to be a permanent arrangement.

Before using this approach, all other options need to be explored and every effort implemented to reach accord—either by BARGAINING or CARING CONCESSION.

Until that gap is bridged, agreeing to disagree allows for mutual respect and trust to exist between both partners while they search for a solution.

Again, attitude is the key! Respect, trust, and forgiveness must be brought to bear on the issue. With objectivity there is a chance for an agreeable solution.

The value of patience throughout this process cannot be overstated. Sometimes only the passage of time can help you gain perspective on an issue. This window of time shouldn't be regarded as a chance for one partner to "wear down" the other one. It is rather an opportunity to allow nurturing and caring to continue in the relationship, with the goal of achieving mutual understanding and appreciation.

A word of warning. If the relationship has not developed, and you do not share a minimal level of respect, trust, and forgiveness, then the chances of staying together with an unresolved, deep conflict are probably slim.

A qualified pastor or professional counselor could potentially help lift you above the forest to get a new glimpse of the trees.

IF ALL ELSE FAILS...
THIRTY QUESTIONS TO ASK BEFORE YOU FINALIZE A DIVORCE

Record your answers on a separate sheet of paper. Be sure to write down your thoughts! The value of "seeing" your ideas and feelings could be life-changing.

1. In one word, why am I considering a divorce?

2. If we were able to relive our married life, what would I do differently?

3. If we were able to live our married life over, what would I want you to do differently? Why?

4. What are the most positive high spots of our marriage to this point?

5. Why did I enjoy dating you?

6. What five to ten areas cause pressure in our marriage? Why?

7. What would I have to do to relieve these pressures?

8. What do I admire most about you?

9. What positive things would I miss most if we divorced?

10. How do I honestly feel about our sex life? Why?

11. What do I enjoy most about sex with you?

12. How do I feel about our ability to communicate? Why?

13. In what five areas do we have the poorest communications? Why?

14. When—in our marriage—did I feel we had the very best communication?

15. How do I really feel about the way we do or don't encourage each other and appreciate each other?

16. How do I feel about the way you think about money?

17. How do my attitudes toward money affect our relationship?

18. What is the biblical standard . . . for the way I am to relate to you? . . . about divorce?

19. How would I describe the ideal marriage? Why?

20. How do I feel when we pray together?

21. How do I feel when I know you are praying for me?

22. How would I feel if you died today?

23. How would our divorce affect my personal self-image?

24. How long has it been since we have had a weekend away from everyone and everything? Why?

25. Being coldly realistic, what would happen to the children if we divorced? To our parents? To our friends? Our company? Our estate?

26. What would be the hardest part of the divorce for me?

27. Do I really want to divorce, or do I really want our relationship to change for the better? In what areas must it change? Why? How?

28. It's easy to blame you for our problems . . . but in all honesty . . . where have I clearly been in the wrong?

29. Would our divorce be "Cutting off my nose to spite my face"?

30. How can this time of pressure, conflict, and hurt be turned into a lesson which will strengthen our marriage over the next fifty years?

CONCLUSION

Congratulations!

You have just completed a powerful step toward demonstrating and securing your married love.

No other earthly relationship has such potential magnitude for reaching and experiencing the height and depth of love and intimacy.

Choosing to love can be demonstrated in everyday, practical ways by giving the gift of respect, trust, and forgiveness.

Now . . . may you climb to the highest peak and enjoy the grandest view of all—your love, your marriage, made possible because YOU made it happen. Together!

—The Authors

P. S. If you would like to dream with us

about reducing divorce by 25 to 50 percent in the next twenty years, write for more information about:

—becoming involved in a Preventing Divorce Team Ministry

—seminars and retreats for preventing divorce

—additional resources for preventing divorce

Write to:

> Greg & Candy McPherson
> P.O. Box 755
> Leavenworth, WA 98826

Welcome aboard!

APPENDIX
PROVEN MARITAL PROBLEM-SOLVING PROCESSES

A. A KEY TO RESOLVING TOUGH ISSUES: ATTITUDE EVALUATION

Each person evaluate and determine where you are.

1. RESPECT

   a. Check the phrases that best describe *your attitude* on this issue.

     _____ Tender and soft
     _____ Critical and harsh

     _____ Understanding and caring
     _____ Do not listen to spouse's needs

     _____ Consider spouse more important than the issue
     _____ The issue is more important than spouse's feelings

_____ Accept spouse's weaknesses

_____ Do not accept spouse's weaknesses

b. Have your spouse check the phrases that best describe *your* attitude on the issue from his or her point of view.

If you do not agree, see if you can discuss why you are disagreeing—and work toward an understanding with respect.

If respect is not strong between you, your foundation will be potentially too weak to reach a satisfactory agreement. You both must feel you respect the other.

Remember: Giving respect is based on value, a sense of worth. Where your treasure is, your heart will be also. When you choose to give higher respect, you will literally treat the other person better.

Do you both agree that your respect for each other on the conflicting issue is solid?

2. TRUST

a. Check the phrases that best describe *your attitude* on this issue.

_____ Share the truth, but try to be sensitive to other's feelings

_____ Share the truth, but probably not as sensitive as needed.

_____ Open and willing to share thoughts/feelings, fears, insecurity, rejection, trust, joy, etc.

_____ Not really open or willing to share thoughts/feelings, fears, insecurity, rejection, trust, joy, etc.

b. Have your spouse check the phrases that best describe *your* attitude on this issue from his or her point of view. If you do not agree, see if you can discuss why you are disagreeing and work toward an understanding with trust.

If trust is not strong between you, your foundation will be—potentially—too weak to reach a satisfactory agreement. You both need to feel that you can trust each other.

Remember: Trust is based on being honest and responsible. When you choose to be honest yet sensitive, and endeavor to demonstrate responsible actions, you build trust.

Do you both agree that your trust level is high and stable regarding this issue?

3. FORGIVENESS

   a. Check the phrases that best describe *your attitude* on this issue.

   _____The hurt and/or hate that might be felt is painful, but must be let go.

   _____The hurt and/or hate that might be felt is too great, and can't be let go.

   _____The relationship is more important than the issue.

   _____The issue is dominant and affects the relationship.

   _____I will not deal with the offense I feel.

   _____The offense needs to be dealt with.

   b. Have your spouse check the phrases that best describe *your* attitude on this issue from his or her point of view.

   If you do not agree, see if you can discuss why you are disagreeing and work toward an understanding with forgiveness. Forgiveness is essential for strong relationships.

   Remember: If you are not able to deal with an offense, it will soon tie you into "emotional knots." You may become critical and negative. To forgive is the only successful way to move toward healing and stability again. You and the relationship can then be healed.

B. FIVE-STEP PROBLEM-SOLVING PROCESS

If discussion does not bring about a reasonable agreement, consider walking through this five-step process.

You may "discover" the workable answer.

STEP # 1
Each person evaluate and determine where he or she is on this chart.

UNRESOLVED CONFLICT[1]

DIFFERENCE OF OPINION ——"SPAT" —— CONFRONTATION
HEATED DEBATE OR ARGUMENT——"QUARREL"——— DIVISION
INTENSE PHYSICAL ANGER ———-"FIGHT"——— REJECTION
HOSTILITY CONFIRMED ————"WAR"——— -SEPARATION

Conflict left unresolved will potentially grow and progress through the steps in the above chart. The ultimate result of unresolved conflict is separation.

STEP # 2 - DEFINE THE DISAGREEMENT

Write down and describe the issue you are trying to resolve.

STEP # 3 - DESCRIBE NEEDS AND HANG-UPS

    A. Who has the need for a solution?
    B. Describe the needs—write them down.

C. Describe what each person is contributing to the disagreement—write it down.

STEP # 4 - DEFINE POTENTIAL SOLUTIONS

Make a list of possible alternatives.

STEP # 5 - AGREE ON A PLAN

Negotiate until you reach a satisfactory agreement.

1. James Fairfield, *When You Don't Agree* (Scottsdale, Penn.: Herald, 1977), p. 19. Used by permission.